FAUNAL

Also by Peter Reading

Collected Poems:
1: Poems 1970-1984
(Bloodaxe Books, 1995)

Water and Waste (1970)
For the Municipality's Elderly (1974)
The Prison Cell & Barrel Mystery (1976)
Nothing For Anyone (1977)
Fiction (1979)
Tom o' Bedlam's Beauties (1981)
Diplopic (1983)
5x5x5x5x5 (1983)
C (1984)

Collected Poems:
2: Poems 1985-1996
(Bloodaxe Books, 1996)

Ukulele Music (1985)
Going On (1985)
Stet (1986)
Final Demands (1988)
Perduta Gente (1989)
Shitheads (1989)
Evagatory (1992)
Last Poems (1994)
Eschatological (1996)

Work in Regress (Bloodaxe Books, 1997)
Ob. (Bloodaxe Books, 1999)
Marfan (Bloodaxe Books, 2000)
[untitled] (Bloodaxe Books, 2001)

Peter Reading

FAUNAL

BLOODAXE BOOKS

ISBN: 1 85224 587 5

First published 2002 by
Bloodaxe Books Ltd,
Highgreen,
Tarset,
Northumberland NE48 1RP.

www.bloodaxebooks.com
For further information about Bloodaxe titles
please visit our website or write to
the above address for a catalogue.

Bloodaxe Books Ltd acknowledges
the financial assistance of Northern Arts.

Cover printing by J. Thomson Colour Printers Ltd, Glasgow.

Printed in Great Britain by
Cromwell Press Ltd, Trowbridge, Wiltshire.

To Wm. Johnston

Acknowledgements

Some of the avifaunal pieces in this book were broadcast by BBC Radio 3. Other material was first published in *Metre, Poetry Review* and *The Times Literary Supplement.*

Contents

'We will now discuss in a little more detail the struggle for existence...'

On Bruny Island, off Tas.,

we were driving along a dirt road
to locate a breeding pair
of Forty-spotted Pardalote
when we damn near hit an Echidna
(Tachyglossus sestosus)
snuffling into the verge grass.

We got out to scrutinise it,
inhale its stink and consider
this marvellous monotreme
and all elegant biodiversity.

Neighbourhood Watch

'...let it profit thee to have heard,
By terrible example, the reward
Of disobedience; firm they might have stood,
Yet fell; remember, and fear to transgress.'
                    MILTON,
                    Paradise Lost

Those loafers, corner-boys, do-nothings, bums,
drones, idlers, layabouts, thugs, loungers, wastrels,
time-wasters, shirkers, ne'er-do-wells, yahoos,
yobs, yobbos, hallions, churls, hobbledehoys,
dossers, delinquents, swads, louts, hooligans,
unemployed tosspots, hoodlums, rowdies, scums,
have got away with too much for too long,
the neighbourhood is going to the dogs.

The PM wants to see the squeegee merchants
(who lurk at traffic lights to accost your windscreens)
eliminated. Beggars he finds repulsive,
offensive to the sensibility –
these 'homeless' people simply are a nuisance
and should be done away with so that decent
members of the community don't see them
and feel distressed.

                    He never gives to beggars,
but once purchased a copy of the *Big Issue*
which caused him a virtuous *frisson* for a week.
He knows it's right to be intolerant
of vagrants – it's appalling that young people
are to be found in grimy sleeping-bags
in decent people's doorways. He will clear
the streets of 'winos', 'alcos', 'dossers', 'addicts'.

– Is there a Third Way? We believe there is.
The welfare system, as we well perceive,
is wasteful and inappropriately addictive.
Social Security benefits encourage
a culture of dependency, you see.

Public expenditure (thus Blair and Schröder,
in 1999, express concern)
has reached the limits of the acceptable.

He'd fine graffiti artists on the spot –
how would you feel if your mother read such things?,
the neighbourhood would be a darned sight better
if thugs like this were fined or put away
and decent folk could stroll the unsullied streets.

The lager louts who kick your garden gate
and bellow down the road on Friday nights
and chuck the orange traffic cones about
and sometimes even take their trousers down
facetiously displaying insolent buttocks,
he thinks should be arrested by stout bobbies,
marched to the nearest cash point and required
to contritely withdraw £100
each and convey it to the officers.
[Which jackass proposition may well prove
more difficult to enforce than to dream up.]

The hallions are more than an aesthetic
displeasure, they represent the end of us;
the hallions are hammering at the door;
the neighbourhood is going to the dogs.
[But more than electoral bluster is required
to arrest the momentum of this gathering maelstrom.]

Field Note

I riffle my notebooks' leaves now at my desk:

A page erased, eroded, foxed, forgotten.

[Untitled]

They sprawl round the pool;
I seek arboreal shade –
        less melanomas.

                *

Last night I dreamed of the red-finned, bronze-girthed Rudd
for which we fished in the Marl Pond when we were blithe.
But now, my brother, I think you are dying –
four-fifths of your stomach to the scalpel,
your back bent double with chemo.

                *

The dark shore white with
Larus atricilla, you,
        child, throwing them bread.

Only the Laughing Gulls, now.

                *

Japanese art buffs
emerge from the Van Gogh show
clutching prismatic cartons
        emblazoned **Vincent**
containing rolled up posters –
the rich harvest molested
        by malign corvids.

That find of *Longisquama insignis,*

oldest known feathered fossil evidence,
from a reptilian creature which most likely
glided between the trees in forest swamps
75 million years pre-*Archaeopterix*
in Central Asia, anticipated birds.

It had a furcula virtually the same
as modern birds, and *wasn't* a dinosaur.

What was the initial function of those feathers
(whose evolution probably antedates
the dinosaur)? Did they develop from scales
for insulation when warm blood arrived?
Or did these nascent plumes burgeon from ridges
along the back, and muscles then develop
in forelimbs, coincident with plumage growth,
enabling first flight?...

Sunt aliquid manes.

Anthropological

We anchored in a bay under the island
and, on our way to shore, pulled alongside
a group of abject natives in a canoe.

These tribes possess no fragment of attire
and go quite naked. Rain was falling hard,
and this, together with the spray combined,
ran down their naked bodies in rivulets.

In another harbour, distant about a league,
a woman, suckling a new-born child,
came alongside the vessel and drifted there
while sleet fell and thawed on her nakedness
and on the tender skin of her bare baby.

These hapless wretches, stunted in their growth,
had hideous faces daubed with gaudy paint,
their skins engrimed with filth, their hair entangled,
their voices harsh, discordant, ululant,
their gestures violent, lacking dignity.
Watching such men, one scarcely can believe
that they are fellow-creatures inhabiting
the same world.

                    It is commonly conjectured
what pleasure life affords to lower species:
how much more reasonably the very same
question may be applied to these barbarians.

At night some five or six of these poor beings,
naked and unprotected from the wind
and lashing rains of this tempestuous climate,
sleep on the wet ground, curled like trembling curs.

Whenever it is low water, they must rise
to harvest shellfish from the rocks; the women,
winter or summer, dive to collect sea eggs,
or, shivering, sit with baited lines to jerk
small fishes from the water into their boats.

Should the putrid carcass of some floating whale
be found, it is a feast, guzzled with relish,
accompanied by a few sour berries and fungi.
Famine is frequent, and, in consequence,
cannibalism and parricide prevail.

No government or head men are there here,
but hostile neighbours, speaking in different thoughts.

Their warfare is occasioned by the lack
of jealous-guarded pitiful resources.

Frontiers reflect past acts of butchery.

Their country is a broken mass of rock
viewed through the gloomy mist of endless storms.

In search of food they are compelled to roam.

To knock a limpet from a rock requires
no towering intellect.

                    Their base condition
is nowise bettered by experience.

They are at once vile and intractable.

Congress Avenue Bridge in Austin, Texas,

Mexican Free-tailed Bats,
Tadaria brasiliensis (mexicana),
over one million of them
at dusk emerging from roost-slots under the span.

They formed a granular trail
dispersing into the dark.
One of the most spectacular
phenomena I have ever been privileged to witness.

I threw the Zeiss in the Colorado River
(after 38 years they were ruined from sea-spray and grit –
I remember, one time, their slithering into a rock-pool
while I was busied banding a Purple Sandpiper)
and then became drunk to celebrate the occasion.

The Sheriff's Department dealt with the peccadillo
(six hours stuck in stir
with a bunch of Mexican kids on a charge of Possession).

When I got out it amounted to two hundred dollars
(Public Intoxication).

Along the river
early next morning (I had the Bausch & Lomb
to replace the Zeiss) a Sora was stalking the reeds.
Overhead, Scissor-tailed Flycatchers
foretold the fall migration.

Cetacean

Out of Fisherman's Wharf, San Francisco, Sunday, early,
our vessel, bow to stern, some sixty-three feet,
to observe Blue Whales – and we did, off the Farallones.

They were swimming slowly, and rose at a shallow angle
(they were grey as slate with white mottling, dorsals tiny and stubby,
with broad flat heads one quarter their overall body-lengths).

They blew as soon as their heads began to break the surface.
The blows were as straight and slim as upright columns
rising to thirty feet in vertical sprays.

Then their heads disappeared underwater, and the lengthy, rolling
expanse of their backs hove into our view – about twenty feet longer
than the vessel herself.

And then the diminutive dorsals
showed briefly, after the blows had dispersed and the heads had
gone under.

Then they arched their backs, then arched their tail stocks ready
for diving.

Then the flukes were visible just before the creatures vanished,
slipping into the deep again, at a shallow angle.

Thanksgiving

That day on the coast of Veracruz,
within a single hour,
into the bright crisp focus
of the Bausch & Lomb 8-42s:
a Magnificent Frigatebird
(adult male, glossy black,
red throat pouch, bifurcate tail)
above a hurricane-shunted
vast sand dune, and, below,
quartering open scrubland,
an Aplomado Falcon
(slate crown, white eyebrow and chest,
black flanks, cinnamon belly),
and, perched on a string of barbed wire,
a Fork-tailed Flycatcher
(black tail-plumes twice its body-length,
black cap, pure white underparts).

And for this I gave, and give, thanks
to *Fregata magnificens*,
to *Falco femoralis*,
to *Tyrannus savana*
and to William Johnston – *¡Amigo!*

Beethovenstraat,

outside the Fidelio Bar
sipping a gelid beer.

Suddenly overhead,
long tails, jet-fighter flight,
skree-ik, skree-ik, skree-ik –
Rose-ringed Parakeets
hurtle above the traffic
(Afro/Asian species,
Psittacula krameri,
feral here, they breed
freely in Vondelpark).

In acknowledgement of which
epiphanic event,
Een ander Amstel, alstublieft.

Lit.

You know that it's time to pack up
when the shelves in the shops are stocked
with titles like *Give Us A Break!*
by an osteopath named Berk,
and *Ashtrays Through The Ages*
by Vladimir Hogsnot-Smoke.

Educative

One day, when I was ten or thereabouts,
the Natural Science teacher, Mrs Hope,
assisted by the *Bug-Eye*, as we fondly
dubbed *Caliban* the Caretaker, turned up
trundling an ancient epidiascope
which she proceeded to plug in, adjust,
and focus until a rectangle of light
was dimly projected on the classroom wall.
Within the bright glow of the apparatus
she conjured a large illustrated book
until an image, furry, indistinct,
became apparent on the impromptu screen.

Children, these are serious times indeed...

It had been, once, a coney, but was now
a distorted, swollen, slimy face with eyes
bulging and blind (not *that* dissimilar
to those of the hapless Janitor).

                    Years on,
the distemper reached an island off the coast
of North Wales where I helped to break the backs
and pitch the bodies of the unfortunate,
infected creatures over the East Face cliff...
(We are all members of the Wildlife Trust.)

Forty more years, a Trustee is defining
Myxomatosis: *Viral disease in rabbits;*
produces fever; lesions of the skin
resembling myxomas; muscoid swelling
of mucous membranes; it exists in nature
in South American species of the genus
Sylvilagus, *and has been introduced*
to parts of Europe and Australia
as a means of rabbit population control...

Ladies and Gentlemen, back in '54,
an article in The Times *of July 1st*
reports that: 'Myxomatosis, this past year,
has extirpated 90 per cent of burrows
in southern England alone. Farmers insist
that this is a virus vital in the control
of rabbits, which do vast amounts of damage –
some £50 million each year. However,
scientists warn that if you disturb the balance...'

[Somehow it seems a long way back to me:
the swollen, mucoid features, bulging, blind;
the conjured image, furry, indistinct;
the dim, projected concept in poor light;
the corrupt corpses of the unfortunate
(we are all members of the Wildlife Trust)
viewed through an ancient epidiascope;
the deluded ramblings of Old Ma Hope.]

From the Chinese

He is a mock sportsman
who slings a dead rat
in his girdle.

He who has
an iron mouth
and bean-curd feet
will not be able
to escape trouble.

He who does not drink
has a negligible wine bill.

Soap (*I.M.*, G.E.)

Joey is outraged at Pacey's advance
but starts to question her reaction.
Henry disappoints Jen by not inviting her to his birthday,
while Tricia makes Marlon's day
and Rosa has an angry confrontation
with Fiona Morris. Gianni, on the other hand,
gets some devastating news from his solicitor.
Meanwhile, Fraser is forced to take drastic action
against his ruthless new landlord and Jamie
hits back at Billy.

But – what's this?!:
Tad gets mad with Paul and Simone
and, before you know where you are,
Mandy visits her dad,
Joel's courting ends in calamity,
Roy is furious to find out
about Scott's underhand dealings
and Bernice questions Zoe's commitment,
so of course Geoff and Doreen
catch Jack and Vera out
and Linda tries desperately
to conceal the truth about Mike's health
even though Tad holds a grudge against Paul and Simone
and Pollard threatens to expose Scott
and the next thing you know is
Danny steams ahead with his plans
to marry the girl of his dreams,
Joe is not happy that Flick played truant,
Ashley considers a shock proposal,
Chris makes plans with Tara's money,
Zak and Cain lay down the law,
Tony is annoyed that Adam stayed the night,
Tim makes things worse for Sinbad,
Mick has a romantic proposition for Susannah,
Felicity stands her ground with Sean,

Joel struggles with his feelings for Dione
(Emily is frankly appalled),
a journalist looks for Nicky di Marco,
Dan continues to harass Melanie
which leads Steve into taking some drastic action,
Tricia realises the truth about Marlon,
Gary embarks on a holiday romance,
Darren is evicted
and the whole fucking schemozzle
ends in a welter of puke, shite and claret.

In Glen Waverley, Melbourne,

over High Street Road, where rush-hour
lasts twenty hours a day
and the pantechnicons hurtle
and honk through exhaust-fume smog,

up on the giant lamp-posts
above the rage of the traffic
a bunch of Sulphur-crested
Cockatoos overwhelm,
the din with harridan skreeches.

And one wonders what early settlers
made of the murderous screams
coming out of virgin forest
where they landed, fearing the worst.

Emission

The Plant disperses plenty no good shit –

sulphuric hailstones drub your washing-lines,
acidulate your long johns, jumpers, jeans.

Faunal

I

...who sat on the rail
nursing a Smith & Wesson *Chief's Special.*

With the percussion,
dove backwards
into the cleanliness of the weir.

[Let us regard with compassionate resign
those unfortunates whom
we shall assuredly join.]

II

If you woke up x hundred years ago,
on a spring morning such as this, maybe
you'd be inclined to conjour in your mind:

What maketh thus this Sparrowy Tribe to twitter?!

III

Looking over the rail
of the fish wharf, Monterey Harbour:
immediately below was a Southern Sea Otter
(Enhydra lutris nereis)
crunching a crab, between bites
resting it on its chest.

Later, at Point Lobos,
another of those remarkable creatures,
this time bashing Mussels to bits
on its chest on a stone anvil which it clutched to
each time it dived
to wrest another mollusc
from the rocks under the floating brown Kelp...

Inconsequential, maybe,
but I have a dead friend
whom I recall on these occasions.

IV

Again the Homeric dream,
Olive and Oleaster,
under which the fallen leaves are scraped
and demise commences.

At Pelee Point

It was decorous that day, Johnston, my friend, to slosh out the vintage
(the Pelee Island white with its label adroitly depicting
a Great Blue Heron) and raise our generous golden bumpers
to the Bald Eagle, American Woodcock, Scarlet Tanager,
Bay-breasted, Chestnut-sided and Blackburnian Warblers,
and commit ourselves to the onset of the autumn migration.

[Untitled]

The small skiff has been rowed
deep into the Great Reed-mace,
the oars are stowed,
the occupant deadly supine
in the clinker planks,
a Bittern, mottled dead-bracken,
bill erect, static, *whoomp-booms*,
and there is autumnal evening precipitation.

Axiomatic

The Sage seems ridiculous
   to the eighth-rate twerp.

   Comfort and warmth
are conducive to love;
   hunger and cold
to theft and thuggery.

Reiterative

Now, beyond hope, I still owe the gods great gratitude.
Marvels are many, mankind among them who navigates oceans,
driven by stormy south-westers, making way through the billows
and surges that threaten to drown and engulf his laborious progress.
And Earth, wearied, wears on, each year turning under the plough.

[Untitled]

Tanker founders,
on slick-black holiday sands
oiled auks flacker.

Brr...

When the telephone
stridently pierces the dark:
'Did I love my Mom enough?
  Whaddabout my Pop?'

Those *Alligator mississippiensis*

delicately copulating in a lagoon
in Aransas, south-east Texas,
their fondling, fumbling under
the surface with sensual claws
and jaws, the joyous writhing
needs neither intellectual
nor moral smartarse envoi.

[Untitled]

In the Library
all seem to have some *purpose*.
I, *per contra*, plot
a visit to the NatWest,
followed by intemperance.

Axiomatic

We take off our shoes;
will we wear them tomorrow?

We can't foretell this morning
what will befall this evening.

When we go to bed
we cannot be sure that we
will rise tomorrow.

When the black leech sticks
to the foot of the egret
he struggles to shake it off
but is unable.

Up in the Chiricahuas,

about 9,000 feet,
a switchback trail through spruce
and pine to a beat-up fire-lookout,
Steller's Jay, Pygmy Nuthatch,
Mexican Chickadee,
impeccable Red-faced Warbler...

Later, *vinum sacrum*
to properly honour this day
of secular *epiphania*.

Port Fairy,

Victoria,
the only mainland colony
of Short-tailed Shearwaters,
dusk before they bullet,
from the day's pelagic foraging,
into the coney burrows
to regurgitate their piscine
mulch in the gapes of fledglings,
no longer at risk from diurnal
predation.

They are silent
as, an inch above our heads,
close enough to ruffle
our hair, their ballistic shades
hurtle towards the fish stink.

Well, we won't experience *that* again in a hurry –
notch it up, therefore, Deborah, while you may.

Bird Lady

Under a pine in Vondelpark
the Bird Lady has fashioned
an impromptu feed-table,
arrives each morning laden
with bags of sunflower seeds
and kibbled maize and proceeds
to feed the feral Rose-rings
(Psittacula krameri,
40 centimetres,
general plumage green,
yellowish underwing,
in male, rose collar encircling
hindneck, nape suffused
bluish) and Alexandrines
(Psittacula eupatria,
58 centimetres,
a group of pristine males,
occiput and cheeks
suffused with bluish-grey,
black stripe through lower cheek,
pink collar encircling hindneck,
red slash on secondary coverts,
massive vermilion bill,
call – a skreeching *kee-ak*),
which, were it not for her
genial dottiness,
would not survive the severe
calorie-wasting winter,
and *we* would be undernourished.

That Nine-banded Armadillo

(Dasypus novemcinctus)
scruttering into the brush
and Prickly Pear of a pathside
in Aransas, south-east Texas,
requires no fancy moral
or intellectual envoi.

In Victoria

When the rafts of Little Penguins
(Eudyptula minor) ascend
through the punishing surf of the ocean
to the Philip Island colony
as the safety of darkness arrives
and they burst from the water and flapper
up to the occupied burrows
where the waiting nestlings clamour
there is laughter and condescension
and the flashing of Nikons and Canons
from the vapid goons who have gathered
to gawp from their raked terrace seats.

Field Note (Everglades)

As elevated nostrils
and eye sockets
of an *Alligator mississippiensis*
slow-motion cruise
across the black channel
a Green Heron
(Butorides virescens)
which has remained fixed
leaning precarious to the water
for fifteen minutes precisely
edges back along its twig
with the choreographed dexterity
of a survivor.

Journal

Of primitive creatures I observed a few,
after we landed at St Jago – large
Aplysia are common. This sea-slug,
grey-yellow coloured, has two antennae
in shape resembling some mammal's ears.
Each side the long foot there's a wide membrane
which, rippling, causes water currents to flow
over the dorsal branchiae.

                    It feeds
on fragile matter. I found in its gut
all sorts of festering slurry. When 'tis jabbed,
this slug emits a purplish fluid, also
stinging secretions rendering it repulsive.

I found, in the same place, *H. sapiens.*

I found, in one part, this grave malady:
General Paralysis of the Insane –
outdated term for tertiary syphilis.

Becalmed, next day, in a *Sargassum* limbo.

One time we passed the night in Punta Alta,
busied myself with palaeontology.
An evening of perfection, calm and clear,
mud-banks and gulls, sandhills, suspended vultures.

I found no fossil but my single self.

We saw a couple of *Zorillas*, or skunks –
odious creatures, far from uncommon here.
They roam by day about the open plain
fearing nor dog nor man, their fetid fluid
inducing nausea and rendering those
polluted by it useless everafter.

Azara says the stink can be discerned
at a league's distance – more than once, indeed,
on the entering of Monte Video Harbour,
breeze being offshore, we have olfactoried it
aboard the vessel. Certainty it is
that even Man rates poor with the *Zorilla*
in this respect of fundamental stench.

When the bull has been dragged to the slaughterplace,
the *matador*, with caution, slashes the hamstrings.
That death-bellow is a sound more eloquent
than any ferocious agony I know.

The struggle now is drawing to a close:
this earth comprises bones and blood; the horses
and riders wallow in gore/faeces slough.

During my sojourn in Bahia Blanca,
awaiting the arrival of our vessel,
three hundred men arrived from the Colorado
under command of Commandant Miranda.

Most of these men were *mansos* Indians
who passed the night here. 'Tis impossible
to conceive of anything more odious
than the hideous vision of their bivouac:
some drank unto profound intoxication;
some gulped the still-steaming blood of slaughtered cattle,
then, vomiting from drunkenness, cast up,
smirching themselves with puke and filthy gore.

Of the Batrachian reptiles, I discovered
only one tiny toad, most singular
in colouration – if we imagine, first,
that it was steeped in blackest ink, and then,
when dry, had been allowed to crawl across
a board fresh-painted bright vermilion,
so as to tint its soles and underbelly,
some notion of its appearance may be gained.

If no nomenclature has been yet applied,
then, surely, it should be *diabolicus*,
for 'tis a toad to preach in the ear of Eve.

Our sleeping place was the Lagoa Marcia.
We passed, at dusk, under a granite steepness
(so common hereabouts) and this terrain
had been for many years the residence
of runaway slaves, who managed to cultivate
a little land atop, and eke a subsistence.

At length they were discovered, and, a posse
of soldiers being sent, the whole were seized,
with th' exception of one old crone, who, rather than
submit herself again to slavery,
dashed herself into pieces from the crag.

After we took fresh vegetables aboard,
December 1833, our vessel
sailed from the Rio Plata, nevermore
to enter its Stygian waters, for Patagonia.
We were infested with insects. As we headed
one evening ten miles off the Bay of San Blas,
vast numerous hordes of butterflies appeared,
far as the telescope could range, and they all drowned.
The sailors cried: 'This is impossible!
'Tis snowing butterflies!' I'm told the species
was *Colias edusa*. I am indebted
to Waterhouse for the naming of these dead.

The deathly stillness of that plain, those dogs

guarding the gipsy tribe of Gauchos, sleeping
beside their campfire, have left in my mind
a memory not soon to be forgotten.

And of all things I've seen and thought and done,
this voyage was my most remarkable.

*

I riffle my notebooks' leaves now at my desk
(they seem to have been laid down so long ago,
like palaeontological deposits) –

'On Chatham Island, I slept one night on shore.
Next morning, glowing heat. I scrambled over
the rough volcanic surface of the ground,
which, taken with the intricacy of barbed thickets,
served to fatigue me greatly. I was amply
rewarded by a strange Cyclopean scene.
Two huge tortoises, each of which, if weighed,
must have been in excess of 200 pounds.
One of them masticated on a cactus,
and, as I drew close, paused to examine me,
then quietly walked away; the other hissed
before withdrawing into its carapace.
The sheer size of these reptiles, their stark context,
surrounded by black lava, leafless shrubs,
and spiky cacti, they seemed, to my fancy,
like creatures roused from antediluvian sleep...'

I riffle my notebooks' leaves now at my desk –

one page is gnarled and stained from salt spray hurled
by the Humboldt Current onto laval rocks:

96

The coastal rocks abound with
great black lizards,
between 3 and 4 feet long; and
on the hills,
another species roams, equally
common.
I saw several of the latter
clumsily run,
or shuffle into their burrows.
#
The aquatic,
great black lizards cling to
sea-pounded rocks,
or swim 100 yards or so from shore
Wonderful
I never saw more hideous-looking
creatures.

And I muse on origins and extirpations.

Endangered

Down on the Gulf Coast of Texas, in the Aransas wetland,
    Johnston and I were observing a posse of Whooping Cranes
(*Grus americana*), Titanium White in crisp focus
    through the Bausch & Lomb, red facial skin, black primaries,
    and a Goddam wingspan of eighty-seven inches.
When they took flight, the trumpets sounded over the marshes,
kerloo kerleeloo, kerloo kerleeloo, kerloo kerleeloo,
and we knew, we knew we would die without seeing the species again.

[Untitled]

Costa del Parvenu:
plenty of foil,
plenty of melanomas.

Laertidean

Drove to the Holy Island over the
    salt-caked causey,
where there were Eiders, Bar-tailed Godwits,
    pale-bellied Brent Geese.
High on the gale-lashed crags above nineteenth-
    century lime-kilns,
Fulmars were nesting: tubular nostrils,
    bull-necks, stiff-winged
gliding and beating. Launching from ledges, they
    lifted, effortless.

And we considered Cuthbert, who, in his
    youth was a sheep herd,
went there as Abbot, then Biscop, and later
    lived as an eremite.
Dane-hordes threatened the monks of Lindisfarne,
    Cuthbert was borne far –
lies now in Durham Cathedral. And we con-
    sidered the crinoids,
Beads of Saint Cuthbert, encrinite fossils.
    And we considered.

of Peleus' son's wrath
I venture to speak

Zeus willed it
but the expedition
caused such grief
with many fine warriors
consigned to the soil

Muse relate how first was engendered the Great Quarrel

the forces were displayed
then were they gathered
each several squadron
all breathing valour

then I the Sacker of Cities
rose up and routed them

then Pandarus broke the truce
then did red-haired Menelaus
rouse his ranks to courage

then did Diomedes war with the Gods
then did the battle-shields' clash continue endless

then Hector bellowed a battle-cry causing the
    Argives to tremble
then he seized up a huge rock from under the massive
    gates of the ramparts
and it tapered into a spear-sharp point
    and its weight was such
that any *ten* men in these enfeebled
    times couldn't raise it
yet for Hector this boulder seemed merely a pebble
    he lifted it lightly
and he braced his legs for a powerful throw
    and he flexed his muscles
then hurtled the missile into the doors which were
    strengthened with stout bars
and the hinges burst and he leapt inside and his
    brow was night-black
then the son of Priam rallied his forces to
    let slip the war-dogs

Then I came to a cottage of stone
at the southern foot of the Long Mynd,
and the masonry's fossils conveyed,
in runes of deposited crinoids
and Silurian brachiopods,
the unending unnerving axiom,
the unending unnerving axiom...

and against the walls a vine thrived,
clustered with generous grapes,
and from its five-fingered leaves
she fondly made me dolmas
with olives and rice and spiced meat,
and we drained red wine and reclined
and I recollected Achilles
and the mists veiling Ilion's ramparts,
and on my departure I heaved
an *Oimoi!* for what I was losing.

then the bellicose Hector threatened our ships and
    huts as he ventured

    seaward through our
    Argive encampment

slaughtering all in his path but he met the
    mass of our forces

when the Achaeans countered him brandishing
    two-spike spear-heads

then the aggressor fell back but with volume
    called on his quailing

troops to return to the warfield – Ilians
Lycians also Dardanians (noted for
    hand-to-hand combat)

though Achaeans stood thick as wall-stones Hector
thought he could rout our armies perforce
since he was sent by the Thunder-One Master of Hērē

so we then slew the captured Dolon
   son of Eumedes
after he'd given us good information
   concerning the Thracians
where they were camped and of their magnificent
   snow-white horses
and we threaded our way through the sable night till we
   found them sleeping
with their priceless gear by their sides and their bold mounts
   tethered beside them
and Rhesus their king in their centre asleep
   with his steeds and his chariot
then the son of Tydeus inspired by Athene and
   wielding his bright blade
slaughtered the slumbering forces from Thrace where they lay

By Amtrak out of Austin to Alpine,
couple of iced Buds in the rattling bar
followed by T-bone and Fort Stockton red.
And through the dust-grained window of the Club Car,
pink Scissor-tails migrating with the fall
and vultures southbound for the borderline
and dried-up gulches, and the tender said:
'I bin this rowt, now, twenny years an all;
nothin much happens in th desert har,
save for th casional flowrin prickly par
an flash-floods thro th dra creek over thar –
I guess ya could say...' but he never finished.
The arid basin, with our speed, diminished;
the glass revealed a season in decline.

Then I sailed | to the Isle | of the Saint | who had shipped |
long ago | with Saint Bren|dan the bold | and his age |
I was told | was two hun|dred-and-twen|ty-five years|
and he spake | in the tones | of a soul | from the kist |
who was one | with the blithe | and his glance | was serene |
and his hair | which was frost | and his beard | which was snow |
were a me|tre in mea|sure and more | and he judged |
that my peo|ple have feu|ded too long | and entrea- |
ted we pon|der the words | of the Lord | who said Ven- |
gance is Mine! | and he railed | how our fa|thers have slain |
and been slain | life for life | interne|cine and *when*
will the hom|icide cease? | and we knelt | at the fringe |
of his beard | and we prayed | and we prayed | and we prayed.|

then while the son of Tydeus
like a lion on the sheepfold
slew a dozen more men of Thrace
I snatched each one by the foot
and unceremoniously flung it
out of the path of the long-maned
stallions we wanted to plunder
and I untethered the thoroughbreds
and tied them together with thongs
and led them away from the blood-field
and upon Athene's advice
we made off for our Argive vessels

and when Hector observed our mighty warrior Patroclus
limp from the fray gouting gore he thrust his bronze spear
   deep through the guts of the son
   of Menoetius of Opus
then the slaying of Priam's son by Achilles was foretold
but Hector scoffed and trod on the fallen Achaean
   and wrenchèd his brazen spear-spike
   out of the corpse's chitterling
and the cadaver soon slipped off the lance and landed
     with its face upwards
     then ensued more wrath

Then we waded at low tide to Hilbre Island;/and we marvelled at scores of thousands of waders – / Sanderling, Knot, Oystercatcher, Redshank, Curlew and Dunlin;/and the giant gull of the north, the hyperborean Glaucous,/glided snow-mantled above the remains of the old lifeboat station;/and there suddenly stooped from a cloud the colour of Blaenau Ffestiniog slate/a Peregrine into a blizzard of wheeling *Calidris alba*/and the falcon hit and we heard the thud and a handful of silvern feathers/whorled in the wind and the great dark raptor rose with the dead meat locked in its talons;/and I said to my friend: 'We will mind this as long as we live.' (He is dead now.)

then each of the Danaan leaders
   ferociously slaughtered his foe
they harried the Trojans just as a ravenous pack
   of wolves does a sheepfold of lambs
snatching the innocents fresh from beneath their ewes' bellies
   whenever the negligent shepherd
abandons his timid charges thus the Danaans
   dealt with the Ilian hordes
   scattering them into rout

Landed on Ynys Enlli, island of
  currents, where we re-

garded a number of myxomatosic
  leporids, mirroring

hominid exit (slime-swollen, tumoral)
  in the next shit-show –

    which, you with certainty know,
    will not be very long now.

then Agamemnon took on Peisander and
  bold Hippolochus

then Atreus' son speared Peisander deeply
  splintring the sternum

then he sworded Hippolochus' arms then the second
  son of Antimachus'
head like a round rock rolled through the awed mob

and I recall how brash Diomedes
    fought with the Gods his
battle-skreech cowed even Aphrodite
    daughter of Great Zeus

and how her lovely skin was incarnadine
when with Iris she left to the left of the field of slaughter

Touched down, Beograd:
slivovitz, crno vino –
    heady days, before
Milosovic rose enraged,
raved and deracinated.

Thence to the Bay of Chesapeake's stubble-fields,
Johnston and I, binoculars tremulous,
    scanning the hoared-land blacked with *Brantas*
    and, in their centre, a single Snow Goose.

then Hector's hurled spear shied off Achilles' shield

the Trojan's body was guarded by bright bronze
yet the Achaean felled our foe with a long lance through the gullet

Landed, at last, among friends;
there in the land I belonged.

Then I regained mine own Penelope.

Afflatious

That cinnamon Nankeen Night Heron
(slender, white nuchal plumes,
black crown, black bill, cream belly)
at roost on an island willow
brushing the brown lake mirror
in Melbourne Botanical Gardens...

And in Texas, that Painted Bunting
(head purple, back green, rump red,
red underparts, dark wings and tail,
bizarrely designed by committee)
picking at tumblegrass seed
in our arid desert garden...

And on Bardsey, off the Welsh coast,
that Wryneck (*Jynx torquilla*)
we caught in the mist-nets, beating
between the bracken and gorse clumps –
the way its head twisted around,
serpentine, primitive,
its vermicular dead-leaf plumage...

And in Badgers Creek, that Lyre Bird
(*Menura novaehollandiae*),
grey-brown, long filmentous tail,
and feet like a couple of garden rakes
grubbing the wet forest leaf-mould...

And on the Mexican border,
that Plain Chachalaca, dull grey,
long glizy green tail tipped white,
guzzling the leaves from the branches,
cha-cha-lac, cha-cha-lac, cha-cha-lac...

And I'd say (if I entertained
such mawkish conceits) that on each

of these afflatious encounters
my soul ascended like that
Skylark I watched as I lay
and dreamed through a summer morning
in a sweet pasture in Shropshire
on an upland when I was younger.